Paleo/Caveman Diet And Gluten Free Recipes Tailored For British Tastes Using Foods Commonly Available In English Stores And Supermarkets

By Budding Books
© Budding Books 2012

Copyright Notice

Introduction:

If you are interested in following the Paleo way of eating, you may already have read a lot of background information into why the human body is designed to function better on a diet as close to that of our hunter gatherer ancestors.

As agriculture has only been around for the past 10,000 years and our bodies have not evolved quickly enough to adapt to the modern diet of dairy and grain-based food, so we are still engineered to be eating a diet of meat, fish, fruit, nuts and vegetables to maintain our bodies in the best possible health.

It's quite astounding how many people are gluten intolerant, and there are thousands more who are unaware they are sensitive to some compounds found within wheat and other grains. Mostly these people will have mild symptoms that show up as headaches or digestive upsets, aching joints, bloating, or a feeling of lethargy, that they just put up with as part of normal life without them realising that grains may be the underlying cause of their health niggles.

Dairy too can cause problems, and there is also a large slice of the population that are lactose intolerant. Our caveman ancestors roamed the land in search of food every day, and they would definitely not have carried a cow over their shoulders just on the off chance they fancied a drink of milk on their journey.

Cheese is often linked with causing migraine headaches, and those who suffer from these terrible debilitating attacks will quite often reduce the frequency and duration of attacks when cheese is eliminated from their diet.

So by following a diet that closely resembles that of our ancestors, we may see a great improvement in our health. This has been proven quite a few times in medical experiments over the years where doctors and scientists have returned volunteers to a more natural diet, and performed numerous tests on their subjects measuring blood pressure, cholesterol lipid counts, lean muscle to fat ratios etc. the results of which all show remarkable improvement for the better.

If you are reading this book because you are interested in following a more natural diet, or because you already know you are gluten or lactose intolerant, then you will find a nice range of recipes on the following pages that will suit your needs.

However, if like me you are British, you may have become aware that the majority of recipe books on the market are aimed at a mainly American readership. There is nothing wrong with this of course, but it can often prove difficult or expensive to source some of the ingredients used in these recipes, as they are not commonly found in British shops or supermarkets.

Knowing what to substitute for buffalo meat, or that cilantro can be swapped for coriander for example, can also slow you down, as will converting the American cup measurements for UK grammes. I personally have no idea what how to weigh out half a cup of sliced mushrooms – do you? And what exactly is a stick of butter?

Now that I mention it – butter, honey and vinegar are not really acceptable for a true, die-hard, strict Paleo enthusiast. But then neither would any processed meats such as bacon or sausage.

Unless you have unlimited time on your hands that you can dedicate to hunting down your prey, searching out and digging up root vegetables from your local park, shooting birds from the sky, and climbing trees to pick fresh nuts and raid bee nests for honey, then I suggest a bit of leeway when it comes to choosing your ingredients for your meals. I have included bacon and sausage in the recipes.

I do apologise if the odd bit of butter creeps into a recipe here or there, but I do love butter and cannot sacrifice it. If you wish to substitute any you find for olive oil, please do so.

I have read that if you stick to eating Paleo for about 85% of the time, this will be great for your health, so for myself I make a little allowance for butter, coffee and a little dark chocolate as an occasional treat.

The overall aim of this book is to give the average British reader a bundle of recipes that use ingredients easily found in shops, supermarkets and farmers markets in the UK and use British measurements. The recipes are based around British staple foods such as beef, chicken, lamb, pork, fish and vegetables, with a few fruit based desserts thrown in for good measure.

There are numerous recipe books and websites that include dessert ideas such as grain-free fruit cakes and cookies, but I find they often use a lot of ground nuts in place of flour, which actually works out to be very expensive. A small bag of ground almonds in my local supermarket was priced at £3.99, and would not have been sufficient for a recipe I was considering making, therefore, I gave up on the idea. Somehow I cannot see Mr Caveman of old stalking a deer with a spear whilst carrying a slice of nut based fruit cake in his pocket.

I also wanted this book to be cost-effective and do-able for people to follow without breaking the bank, so for this reason I have not included any breakfast bars, biscuit replacements, or cake substitutes that use expensive ingredients. Hence my preference for more naturally occurring, and cheaper, fruit based desserts.

Time is precious too, so the recipes have been chosen for their ease of preparation and/or cooking time, which means you will not be spending hours in the kitchen slaving over a hot stove.

So what are you waiting for? Lets get stuck in….

Contents:

Rosemary Chicken With Tomato Sauce

Spicy Chicken with Vegetable Sauce

Mushroom-Stuffed Chicken

Moroccan-Style Chicken With Carrot & Orange Salad

Lamb Dishes

Braised Lamb

Warm Lamb Salad

Fruity Lamb Tagine

Roast Hogget

Greek Lamb Stew

Spicy Lamb Curry

Cooking Mackerel And Other Oily Fish.

Salmon Burgers

Smoked Salmon With Prawns, Horseradish & Lime Vinaigrette

Baked Salmon With Fennel & Tomatoes

Charred Salmon With Fennel & Olive Salad

Mackerel & Beetroot Salad

Barbecued Mackerel With Ginger, Chilli & Lime Drizzle

Smoked Mackerel With Quick Grilled Ratatouille

Mackerel With Warm Cauliflower & Caper Salad

Grilled Mackerel With Orange, Chilli & Watercress Salad

Sardines Stuffed With Orange Slices & Bay Leaves

Grilled Sardines With Cherry Tomatoes, Rocket & Fennel

Winter tuna Niçoise

Sauces Condiments and Crudités

Anchovy Dip

Guacamole

Basil And Spinach Pesto

Parsley Pesto

Coriander Pesto

Gluten-Free Desserts That Are Paleo Friendly And Not Too Expensive!

Sweet Grilled Oranges

Baked apple

Baked Apple With Butter

Spiced Peaches

Warm Fruit Compote

Breakfast

Breakfast is often considered the most difficult meal of the day to adapt to the Paleo way of eating, and for the gluten-free dieter too when you consider the traditional breakfast choices of cold cereal with milk, toast with butter and jam, or porridge.

You don't have to go too far back in our history to see we ate much healthier choices of breakfast. The traditional full English breakfast for example is still eaten today, and was the staple breakfast of our Victorian ancestors, but today it is usually reserved for the weekend when we have more time to prepare and eat it at our leisure.

However time pressed we are during the week, we could still manage to rustle up a modified version of a cooked breakfast with a little planning. Boiled eggs can be prepared while you take your morning shower for example, or you could poach some fish in a frying pan with a little water while you are dressing.

If you are really pressed for time in the morning, why not have some ready prepared breakfast items that you can grab and take with you to work. Hard boiled eggs, small packets of mixed nuts or trail mix, left over cold cuts of meat can be popped into a sandwich bag and carried with you. My particular favourite is a slice of cold vegetable frittata with a small tub of tomato salsa to dip into. Delicious!

I have have included a recipe for gluten free granola and a muesli-type breakfast for those people who really miss their morning cereal. You can eat these with a little coconut milk, almond milk, or with a splash of fresh orange juice if you wish. The granola recipe is also nice eaten dry as a snack.

Some of the cooked breakfast recipes here can be prepared in advance, then stored in the fridge and reheated in the microwave for a delicious and quick breakfast.

Full English Breakfast – Paleo Style

4 rashers good quality lean unsmoked back bacon
4 portabello mushrooms
12-16 cherry tomatoes
6 tsp olive oil
2 good-quality free-range pork sausages
2 free-range eggs
1 handful fresh berries (whatever is in season)

Lay the bacon, mushrooms and tomatoes on a foil-lined tray. Brush the tops of the mushrooms with 3 tsp of the oil. Set aside. Heat the grill to very hot. Lay the sausages on a small foil-lined tray (do not prick the sausages). Grill for about 10 minutes until cooked, turning occasionally. Poach or fry the eggs gently until the whites are set and the yolks are still runny.
Place the tomatoes, bacon and mushrooms under the grill for 3-4 minutes without turning. Drain everything on kitchen paper.

Arrange everything on a plate and serve with the fresh berries to follow at room temperature.

Spinach Mushrooms with Bacon, Egg and Pesto

Ingredients:
1 tbsp olive oil
2 Portobello mushrooms, stalks trimmed
2 rashers smoked streaky bacon
150g/5½oz baby spinach leaf
5 tbsp water
2 free-range egg yolks
Salt and freshly ground black pepper

For the pesto sauce
55g/2oz baby spinach leaves
3 tbsp olive oil
1 garlic clove
100g/3½oz pine nuts
Salt and ground black pepper

Preheat the grill to high.
Heat the olive oil in a small frying pan over a medium heat.
Wrap one strip of bacon around each mushroom and seal with a toothpick. Add the wrapped mushrooms to the frying pan and cover with a sheet of foil, or a lid if your pan has one. Cook for about six minutes, shaking the pan occasionally. Remove from the heat once the mushrooms are cooked, and set aside.

Place the spinach in a microwave-safe bowl with the water. Cover with cling film and cook in the microwave on full power for two minutes, or if you prefer, steam in a pan gently. Remove and set aside.

To make the pesto, place the 55g/2oz spinach, olive oil, garlic and pine nuts in a food processor and blend together. Season, to taste, with salt and ground black pepper and transfer to a serving bowl.

Place the wilted spinach on top of the cooked mushrooms and place an egg yolk on top of each. Season, to taste, with salt and freshly ground black pepper and place under the grill for one minute, or until the yolk is cooked to your liking. To serve, place the mushrooms on a plate and drizzle with pesto.

Easy Ratatouille With Poached Eggs

Ingredients
1 tbsp olive oil
1 large onion, chopped
1 red or orange pepper, deseeded and thinly sliced
2 garlic cloves, finely chopped
1 tbsp chopped rosemary
1 aubergine, diced
2 courgettes, diced
400g can chopped tomatoes
4 large eggs
Handful basil leaves

Heat the oil in a large frying pan. Add the onion, pepper, garlic and rosemary, and then cook for 5 minutes, stirring frequently, until the onion has softened. Add the aubergine and courgettes, and then cook for 2 minutes more.
Add the tomatoes, then fill the can with water, swirl it around and tip into the pan. Bring to the boil, cover, then simmer for 40 minutes, uncovering after 20 minutes, until reduced and pulpy.
Make 4 spaces for the eggs in the ratatouille. Crack an egg into each hole and season with black pepper. Cover, then cook for 2-5 minutes until set as softly or firmly as you like. Scatter over the basil and serve.

Can be frozen without eggs. Try making enough for 3 days worth of breakfast, and store in the fridge to be reheated for breakfast – always cook the eggs fresh.

Spicy Tomato Baked Eggs

1 tbsp olive oil
2 red onions, chopped
1 red chilli, deseeded and finely chopped
1 garlic clove, sliced
Small bunch coriander, stalks and leaves chopped
separately
2 400g cans cherry tomatoes
4 eggs

Vary this dish by flavouring the simple tomato
sauce with whatever you have to hand - curry
powder, pesto or fresh herbs

Heat the oil in a frying pan that has a lid, then
soften the onions, chilli, garlic and coriander
stalks for 5 minutes until soft. Stir in the
tomatoes, and then bubble for 8-10 minutes until
thick. Can be frozen for 1 month.
Using the back of a large spoon, make 4 dips in
the sauce, and then crack an egg into each one.
Put a lid on the pan, and then cook over a low
heat for 6-8 minutes, until the eggs are done to
your liking. Scatter with the coriander leaves and
serve.

This dish can be made in bulk and a portion
reheated for breakfast, but remember to cook the
eggs fresh each day.

Minty Salmon & Broccoli Frittata

1 large head broccoli, cut into florets
2 skinless salmon fillets
1 tbsp olive oil
A small handful mint, finely chopped
8 eggs, beaten

Boil the broccoli pieces for 4 minutes until everything is tender. Drain well. Meanwhile, place the salmon fillets in a microwaveable dish, splash with a little water, then cover in cling film and microwave on High for 2½ minutes until the fish flakes.
Heat the grill. Flake the salmon into large chunks and poke amongst the broccoli. Stir the mint and some seasoning into the eggs, and then pour into a frying pan pan. Leave for 6 minutes over a low heat until the sides are set and just the centre is a little wobbly, then flash under the grill to set completely and brown. Serve in wedges with a big green salad on the side, or chill and eat slices cold for breakfast.

Tenderstem Broccoli with Sautéed Onions & Bacon

300g Tenderstem broccoli, ends trimmed
1 tsp olive oil
1 onion, finely chopped
140g streaky bacon, chopped
2 garlic cloves, finely chopped

Cook the broccoli for 3 minutes in boiling salted water. Drain, run under cold water until completely cooled, then set aside.
Heat the oil in a large frying pan. Add the onion and bacon. Cook on a medium heat for about 10 minutes, adding the garlic halfway through, until the bacon is crisp and the onions are soft and golden.
Add the broccoli to the pan, and then toss through to coat in the oil. Cook for a couple more minutes until the broccoli is completely heated through. Season with pepper, and then serve immediately.

Breakfast Devilled Eggs

Devilled eggs have to be the simplest breakfast item you can make in advance.
Traditionally these little gems are made by hard boiling eggs, and once cooled remove the shell, slice lengthways in half, then remove the egg yolk to mix with a little mayonnaise and a touch of mustard to give it some kick. Then you refill the egg whites with the mixture, chill and serve.

You can vary the filling to make the dish more versatile. Use these tasty combinations:

Bacon treat: Mix the egg yolk with mayonnaise, mustard and finely chopped cooked crispy bacon. Sprinkle with a little fresh chopped parsley.

Crunchy garden salad: Mix the basic yolk and mayo combination with a little chopped red pepper and spring onion.

Spicy eggs: Mix the basic yolk, mayo and mustard combination with a little lemon juice, ground cumin and cayenne pepper to taste.

French style: Mix the yolks with a little mayonnaise, Dijon mustard, and chopped fresh dill.

Gluten Free Granola

This will make about 20 portions, but please remember that this mixture is quite calorific so do go easy on your portion size. It's surprising how filling this mixture is, so you will find you will eat much less than a normal portion of cereal to be full and satisfied until lunch.

You can adjust the ingredients in this mix to suit your particular tastes, substitute one sort of dried fruit for another to give the mix some variety each time you make a batch. Changing the cinnamon to another sweet spice will also give the flavour a fresh twist. Try substituting for ground mixed spice, or ground ginger for example. The idea is to keep the base of sliced almonds and coconut flakes as the main ingredients.

200g flaked almonds
80g coconut flakes
125g chopped walnuts
125g chopped macadamia nuts
65g raisins
80g chopped dates
4 tablespoons olive oil
6 tablespoons runny honey
2 teaspoons ground cinnamon

Preheat the oven to 140C/275F. Mix all the dry ingredients except the dates in a large mixing bowl until well combined.

Put the olive oil and honey into a small microwave safe bowl and heat gently until the honey has melted.

Stir the honey and oil mixture into the fruit and nut mixture and combine well to evenly coat.

Divide the mixture between two baking trays and spread out into thin layers.

Bake for around 35 minutes stirring occasionally until the mix starts to turn golden and a little crispy. It will become more crisp as it cools down.

Remove from the oven and transfer to a mixing bowl. Mix in the dates and leave to cool completely before storing in an airtight container.

Gluten Free Muesli

This is a tasty combination of fruit, nuts and seeds that is nice and chewy, and will keep you topped up with energy all morning.

This makes about 20 portions – again this is quite high in calories, but is so filling you will not need to eat much to fill you up.

75g flaked almonds
60g chopped Brazil nuts
70g sunflower seeds
55g pumpkin seeds
240g coconut flakes
200g chopped dried apricots
200g raisins

In a dry frying pan over a medium heat, lightly toast the almonds, Brazil nuts, sunflower and pumpkin seeds for around 3 minutes, stirring often, until golden. Remove from heat and leave to cool.
Combine the toasted seeds and nuts with the remaining ingredients and mix well. Transfer to an airtight container.

This mix is particularly nice served with a little orange juice and some grated apple.

Ham is not just for holidays. Buy fresh or partially cooked. If you buy fresh, soak to remove salt before cooking and trim the fat for a tender cut of meat. If you want to have a go at cooking your own ham joint, follow the instructions below.

How to Cook Ham

Ham is one of those foods that can pair with a lot of side dishes for a great meal. But, many people avoid it because of the salt.
There are a variety of ways to buy ham. Many people buy it partially cooked or fully cooked. This is fine, but you have a higher sodium count. The flesh is pink to dark pink. These types of hams don't require much preparation. You simply warm them up before eating. For the partially cooked ham, you will have to cook it for longer.

To cook your Ham
Before cooking, soak your ham overnight in water to remove as much of the salt as you can. Remove the skin entirely. Then, trim the fat to about half an inch. You don't want to remove it all or it can dry out your ham while cooking. Many marinate their ham with pineapples and spices for flavour. If you want to add a glaze, allow the ham to begin to cook first and then splash it on.

A ham bakes slowly just like a turkey. Place it in a medium hot oven for a couple of hours. Place the fat side up (for better cooking and more moisture) in a roasting pan.
Ensure the ham is cooked right through before removing from the oven.
Before cutting the ham, let it rest on the side for about 20 minutes.

Storing Ham
If you buy a fresh ham, cook it within a couple of days. You don't want it sitting in your fridge for too long or it will be no good. After cooking, you can cut it up and freeze it for about a month with good flavour results. A whole ham can be frozen for three months.

The following section has some tasty and quick recipes using pork.

Spiced Pineapple Pork

2 tsp vegetable oil
4 pork steaks, trimmed of excess fat
1 tsp tomato purée
432g can pineapples rings in juice, drained, but juice reserved
½ tsp chilli powder
1 tsp Chinese five-spice powder
Coriander leaves, to serve

Add the oil to a large non-stick pan, season the steaks well, then fry for 5 minutes on each side until golden and almost cooked through. Mix the tomato purée and most of the pineapple juice in a bowl.
Add the pineapple rings to the pan and let them caramelise a little alongside the pork. Add the chilli and five-spice to the pan, then fry for 1 min until aromatic. Tip in the juice mix and let it bubble around the pork and pineapple for a few minutes until slightly reduced and sticky.
Sprinkle with coriander, and serve with Chinese greens.

Sticky Slow-Roast Belly of Pork

1.3kg piece pork belly, boned, rind left on and
scored (ask your butcher to do this)
2 tsp sunflower oil
1 tsp white peppercorns, crushed
3 large onions, sliced
2-3 tbsp clear honey
2 tsp ground cumin
1 red chilli, deseeded and chopped

Heat oven to 180C/fan 160C/gas 4. Lay the pork,
skin-side up, on a rack in a roasting tin. Trickle
with a little oil, and then lightly press on the
crushed peppercorns and a sprinkling of coarse
sea salt. Place in the oven, then cook for 1 hr.
Remove from the oven and baste with the juices.
Continue to cook for a further 1½ hrs, basting
every 20 minutes.
Put the sliced onions in the roasting tin under the
pork. Mix the honey together with the cumin and
chilli, brush it over the pork, and then increase
the oven to 200C/fan 180C/ gas 6. Cook for a
further 30-40 minutes, basting occasionally, until
caramelised with a rich, golden glaze over the
pork. Once cooked and tender (this can be easily
tested by piercing the flesh with a knife), remove
pork from the oven, then leave to rest for 10-15
minutes.
While the pork is resting, heat the tin on the stove
with the onions, adding 2 tbsp water. This will
lift any residue from the pan, creating a moist

cooking liquor. Season the onions with salt and pepper, and then divide between 6 plates. Carve pork into 6 portions, and then serve on top of the onions. Pour any remaining liquor over and serve with Pumpkin mash.

Pork, Apple & Sage Burger With Caramelised Onions

900g minced pork
1 onion, finely chopped
1 cooking apple, peeled and finely grated
1 egg
Handful sage

Caramelised onion
3 onions, sliced
2 tbsp honey
Olive oil

To caramelise the onions, cook them with the honey and a little olive oil over a very gentle heat for 30-40 minutes, stirring occasionally. Meanwhile, mix all the burger ingredients together in a bowl and season well. Shape into four burgers, then fry over a medium heat for 6-7 minutes each side until cooked in the middle. Serve on toasted buns with the caramelised onions, a green salad and chunky chips.

Roast Loin Of Pork

Olive oil
1.3kg pork loin, boned and rolled
Sea salt
3 eating apples, cut into wedges
400ml vegetable or chicken stock

Heat the oven to 240C/fan 220C/gas 9. Lightly
oil a roasting tin and put it in the oven to get hot.
Season the skin of the pork with sea salt, then put
the joint in the hot tin and roast for 20 minutes.
Reduce the heat to 190C/fan 170C/gas 5 and
roast for a further 30 minutes per 500g. Increase
the heat to 240C/fan 220C/gas 9 and cook for a
final 10 minutes to get a really crisp and golden
crackling.
Take the pork from the tin and rest in a warm
place before carving into slices. Meanwhile,
drain the excess fat from the roasting tin onto a
baking tray. Add the apples to the hot fat, turn to
coat all over and roast for 10 minutes. Take out
and keep warm.
Put the roasting tin directly over a low heat,
slowly add the stock, stirring well and letting it
all bubble together until you have a gravy.
Season and sieve into a jug.
Serve the pork with the roasted apples and gravy.
To get good, crunchy crackling you need to score
the skin well with a very sharp knife or, better
still, ask the butcher to do it for you.

Three-Hour Pork Belly

2 tbsp fennel seeds
1 tsp black peppercorns
1 small bunch thyme leaves
3 garlic cloves
3 tbsp olive oil
1.5-2kg/3lb 5oz-4lb 8oz piece boneless pork belly, skin scored
2 lemons

Toast the fennel seeds and peppercorns in a dry frying pan for a couple of minutes. Pound them together in a pestle and mortar with some flaked sea salt, the thyme and garlic to make a paste. Mix with 2 tbsp olive oil and rub all over the flesh of the pork. Cover and chill, leaving to marinate for a few hours or overnight.
When ready to cook, rub the skin of the joint with plenty of salt and 1 tbsp more olive oil. Sit on a wire rack in a roasting tin and roast at 200C/180C fan/gas 6 for 30 minutes. After this time, squeeze the lemons over the skin and turn the heat down to 180C/ 160C fan/gas 4. Roast for a further 2 hours. Finally, turn the heat back up to 220C/ 200C fan/gas 7 and give it a final blast for another 30 minutes or so, to finish the crackling. Allow to rest somewhere warm for 20 minutes. Carve up into chunks or slices and serve with the braised cabbage.

Quick Pork With Spring Greens

2 tbsp olive oil
4 boneless pork loin steaks, each weighing about
140g/5oz
2 garlic cloves, crushed
A generous pinch of dried chilli flakes
140g shredded spring greens

To cook the pork, heat the oil in a deep frying
pan that's big enough to fit the greens later.
Season the steaks all over with salt and pepper
and fry over a medium heat for 3-4 minutes on
each side until golden brown. Remove from the
pan and keep hot on a warmed plate or in a low
oven.
To wilt the greens, tip the garlic and chilli flakes
into the same pan and cook for about 30 seconds
until sizzling but not browned, then pour in 5
tablespoons water and toss in the greens. Simmer
for 4-5 minutes until the greens wilt. Stir in any
juices from the pork and continue stirring until
everything's hot. Serve a mound of greens topped
with a steak and any juices.

20-Minute Pork Pan-Fry

500g pork tenderloins fillet
2 tsp dried rosemary
3 tbsp olive oil
250g chestnut mushrooms, sliced
1 fat garlic clove, finely chopped
300ml vegetable stock

Cut the pork diagonally into finger-thick slices.

Tip the rosemary into a large plastic food bag,
add some salt and pepper and the pork, and toss
until the meat is well coated.

Heat 2 tablespoons of the oil in a large wide
frying pan. Add the pork and fry for about 3-4
minutes until nicely browned on both sides,
turning once. Remove from the pan.
Fry the mushrooms: Heat the remaining oil in the
pan, tip in the mushrooms and fry until they start
to soften, about 2 minutes. Sprinkle in the garlic
and return the pork to the pan.
Stir in the stock and bring to the boil. Simmer for
5 minutes or until the pork is cooked.

Mustard Pork With Spinach

Olive oil
Pork tenderloin fillet, about 300g, fat completely
trimmed and sliced
½ tbsp wholegrain mustard
100ml chicken stock
½ lemon, juiced
A small bunch parsley, chopped
200g spinach

Heat a large non-stick frying pan until hot and
add 1 tsp olive oil. Quickly brown the pork slices
all over in batches and scoop out. Add the
mustard and chicken stock, bring to a simmer.

Return the pork to the pan and simmer for 4-5
minutes until just cooked through. Season and
add the lemon juice and parsley. Meanwhile
steam the spinach, divide between 2 plates then
top with the pork and sauce.

Spicy Pork & Aubergine

1½ tbsp olive oil
2 onions, sliced
1 small aubergine (about 250g/9oz), trimmed and diced
500g lean pork fillets, trimmed of any fat and sliced
2 sweet red peppers, seeded and cut into chunky strips
2-3 tbsp mild curry powder
400g can plum tomatoes
150ml water

Heat the oil in a large non-stick frying pan with a lid. Tip in the onions and aubergine and fry for 8 minutes, stirring frequently, until soft and golden brown.
Tip in the pork and fry for 5 minutes, stirring occasionally, until it starts to brown. Mix in the pepper strips and stir-fry for about 3 minutes until soft.
Sprinkle in the curry powder. Stir-fry for a minute, and then pour in the tomatoes and water. Stir vigorously, cover the pan and leave the mixture to simmer for 5 minutes until the tomatoes break down to form a thick sauce (you can add a drop more water if the mixture gets too thick). Season with salt and pepper.

Mustard Pork & Apples

4 pork steaks, approx 140g/5oz each, trimmed of
excess fat
1 tbsp oil
2 eating apples, cored and cut into eight
1 onion, halved and sliced
Small handful sage leaves, torn, or 2 tsp dried
100ml/3½ fl oz chicken or ham stock
2 tsp Dijon mustard or wholegrain mustard

Rub the pork steaks with a little oil and season
with pepper and salt to taste. Heat a large frying
pan and fry the steaks for 2 minutes on both sides
until golden. Transfer to a plate. Adding a little
more oil to the pan, fry the apples, onions and
sage for 5 minutes or until the apples have
softened.
Pour in the stock and spoon in the mustard, then
return the pork to the pan and simmer for 10
minutes until the sauce has reduced by about a
third and the pork is cooked through. Serve with
vegtables.

Herbed Pork Fillet With Roast Vegetables

4 medium parsnips, peeled and quartered
lengthways
1 butternut squash (about 650g/1lb 7oz), peeled,
seeded and cut into chunks
2 red onions, each cut into 8 wedges
1 tbsp olive oil
Grated zest of 1 lemon
2 tsp pork seasoning or dried mixed Italian herbs
500g lean pork tenderloins, in one or two pieces
1 medium Bramley apple
400ml hot chicken stock

Preheat the oven to 200C/ gas 6/fan 180C. Put all
the vegetables into a roasting tin. Drizzle with the
olive oil, season with salt and pepper, and then
toss everything together.
On a plate, mix together the lemon zest and pork
seasoning or herbs. Roll the pork tenderloin in
the mixture, and then put it on top of the
vegetables. Roast for 40 minutes.
Peel and core the apple and cut it into chunks.
Scatter the pieces into the roasting tin, then pour
in the hot stock and cook for a further 15-20
minutes. Slice the pork, arrange on a platter with
the vegtables, then spoon the pan juices on top.

Pork With Pears

1 tbsp sunflower oil
2 red onions, roots trimmed and cut into eighths
2 large pears, quartered and cored (leave the skin on)
Few sprigs rosemary, leaves roughly chopped
4 pork steaks, about 175g/6oz each, trimmed of excess fat

Heat the oil in a roasting tin on the hob (use 2 rings), then add the onions, pears, most of the rosemary and seasoning. Fry for 5 minutes or until just starting to caramelise.
Season the pork, then arrange among the vegetables and fry for 5 minutes, turning halfway until golden and cooked through. Scatter with the remaining rosemary, and then serve.

Pork Chops With Aubergine

1 tbsp olive oil
1 medium aubergine, cut into small cubes
1 tbsp lemon or limejuice
1 tsp honey
400g can chopped tomatoes with garlic
Handful basil leaves, torn
4 boneless pork chops

Heat the oil in a large saucepan, tip in the aubergine then fry over a medium heat for 5 minutes until soft and golden. Pour in the lemon or limejuice. Once the bubbling subsides, stir in the honey, followed by the tomatoes, basil and seasoning to taste. Stir well and cook over high heat for 5 minutes, until the sauce has thickened. Meanwhile, heat the grill to medium and season the pork. Place the chops under the grill for 15 minutes, turning halfway, until golden and cooked through. Serve the chops with the aubergines on the side.

Pork & Peach Kebabs With Little Gem Salad

500g lean pork fillet, trimmed of any fat
2 peaches
1 lemon
2 tbsp clear honey
2 Little Gem lettuces
100g bag watercress
2 tbsp olive oil
1 tsp Dijon mustard

Soak eight wooden skewers in cold water for at least 5 minutes. Cut the pork into large cubes. Halve and stone the peaches, then cut into chunks. Grate the zest from half the lemon and squeeze out the juice. Reserve 1 tbsp of the juice, and then mix the remainder with the zest and honey. Alternately thread the pork and peach slices onto the skewers. Brush all over with the honey and lemon mix, then grill or barbecue for 10-12 minutes, turning regularly, until cooked. Separate the lettuce leaves and mix with the watercress. Whisk the reserved lemon juice with the olive oil, mustard and a little seasoning. Toss with the salad leaves and serve with the kebabs.

Cooking with Beef

There is hardly any food finer than good quality beef, and the ultimate beef dish we all love is a nice, juicy steak! But there are a lot of people who are afraid of cooking steak, so shy away from giving it a proper go.

Don't just keep eating prime steak for restaurant meals on special occasions. Use these tips to prepare your own steak at home.

How to Cook Steak

Choosing your Beef

Steaks come from a variety of cuts of beef. You have T-bone steaks, porterhouse, filet mignon, round steaks, skirt steaks, etc. each has a slightly different look depending on where it comes from in the cow grand design. Obviously, thicker steaks are going to take longer to cook while thinner ones will need much attention to make sure that they don't dry out.

* Prime – These steaks have the greatest amount of marbling (streaks of fat amid lean meat). Marbling makes a steak juicier because the fat helps to keep the meat tender during cooking.
* Choice – This is the next step down. This is the meat you get from the butcher counter in the supermarket. There is still some marbling but not as much.

* Select – You choose this meat yourself in that section of the supermarket. You can still make a great steak but the meat is leaner with little to no marbling.

Preparing your steak

Now that you've chosen the steak you want, here are some tips for getting it ready. You can marinade your steak. Whatever mixture you choose, let it sit in the fridge for at least thirty minutes. This allows the marinade to permeate the meat and also for the meat fibres to break down making for a more tender steak.

Cooking your Steak

You can cook steak several ways. Let's start with grilling.

Choose a steak that has a lot of marbling throughout the meat like a rib eye steak. This will be tender on the grill due to the melting of the fat in the meat. Also, steaks with bones like the T-bone and Porterhouse are also great grilling steaks.

Make sure your grill is hot before adding the steak. Wipe any excess marinade off to prevent flame ups. Cook to desired doneness on each side and then remove. Allow the meat to rest before cutting.

Another way to seal in the juices is through searing and roasting. Use a hot frying pan to begin cooking your steak. This will leave a great looking crust on it. Cook a couple of minutes on each side to set the crust.

Next, place the entire pan in a hot oven to continue cooking (but only if you have a pan with a metal handle, and remove the pan from the hot oven with an oven glove). It won't take long (about five or so minutes depending on thickness) to cook the steak to medium. If you want a well-done steak, leave it in at least twice as long.

Peppered Beef Steak

Ingredients
200g/7oz sirloin steak
1 free-range egg, beaten
2 tsp ground black pepper
1 tbsp olive oil

Dip the steak in the beaten egg and sprinkle with the pepper to coat.
Heat the olive oil in a non-stick frying pan and fry the steak for four minutes on each side, or until cooked to your liking.

Leave the steak aside to rest for five minutes before serving.

Barbecued Fajita Steak

4 beef steaks, preferably rib-eye, approx
250g/9oz each

For the marinade
Juice 6 limes
2 tbsp olive oil
4 garlic cloves, crushed
2 tsp dried oregano
4 tsp ground cumin
2 tsp freshly ground black pepper
Small bunch coriander, finely chopped

Mix all the marinade ingredients in a bowl. Lay
the steaks in a shallow dish or tray, and then pour
over the marinade. Turn to coat the steaks all
over in the mix, and then allow to stand for at
least 1 hour, or cover and chill for up to 24 hrs.
Heat the barbecue. When it is hot, wipe any
excess marinade from the steaks, and then cook
for 3 minutes on each side for medium-rare or
longer if you prefer it more cooked. Allow the
steak to rest for 5 minutes, then cut into thick
slices.

To serve, wrap in large iceberg lettuce leaves and
top with fried onions and peppers. Roll up and
enjoy!

Steak With Grilled Peppers & Coriander Salsa

2 small fillet steaks, trimmed of any fat
Olive oil
2 tsp ground cumin
1 red pepper, thickly sliced
1 yellow pepper, thickly sliced
1 green chilli, seeded and chopped
½ onion, finely chopped
Handful coriander, chopped

Rub the steaks with 1 tsp oil and 1 tsp of the
cumin and season. Drizzle the pepper slices with
1 tsp of oil. Griddle the peppers on both sides for
a few minutes until tender. Blitz the rest of the
cumin, the green chilli, onion, and coriander in a
food processor with enough water to make a
saucy consistency. Season.
Barbecue or griddle the steak for 3 minutes on
each side. Rest for 3 minutes, then serve with the
peppers and sauce.

Quick Beef Stew

Ingredients
1 tbsp olive oil
½ red onion, finely chopped
1 garlic clove, crushed
85g/3oz beef fillet, chopped
½ beef tomato, de-seeded and chopped
1 tbsp tomato purée
2 tbsp boiling water
1 large handful spinach leaves
Salt and black pepper
1 tsp sesame seeds

Heat the olive oil in a pan and lightly fry the
onion and garlic for 3-4 minutes, or until softened
but not coloured. Add the beef pieces and fry for
2-3 minutes, or until the beef is brown.
Add the chopped tomato, tomato purée and water
to the pan, stirring well. Reduce to a simmer and
cook for 1-2 more minutes, or until the beef is
cooked through, then add the spinach. Cook for
1-2 minutes, or until the spinach is wilted, then
season with salt and black pepper.
To serve, spoon the stew into a serving bowl and
garnish with the sesame seeds.

Sloppy Joe Bake

Note: Only make this dish with really good quality lean minced beef, and not the cheap frozen stuff you can buy. The cheaper the mince, the more fat will run off which makes the dish too greasy.

500g pack lean minced beef
2 onions, roughly chopped
2 tsp olive oil
2 tsp ground cumin
1-2 tsp mild chilli powder
400g can chopped tomatoes
600ml beef stock

Brown the mince in a non-stick pan for a few minutes, and then tip into a bowl. Whiz the onions in a food processor until finely chopped (or roughly grate if you don't have one). Tip into the pan with the oil, and then cook for 2-3 minutes until soft. Add the spices, cook for 1 min. Return the mince to the pan with the tomatoes and stock, and then bring to a boil. Simmer for 20 minutes.

Home Made Beef Burgers

Ingredients
1kg/2¼lb minced beef
1 large onion, grated
3 tbsp fresh parsley and thyme
Salt and pepper, to taste

Preheat the barbecue or grill to hot.
Place all the ingredients in a large bowl and mix together with a fork.
With wet hands, shape the meat into flattish round burger shapes of an equal depth to ensure even and thorough cooking.
Cook on the barbecue for approximately 5 minutes on each side - the burgers should be brown in the middle as well as on the outside.
Test one by cutting in half.

This mixture can also be rolled into small, bite-size meatballs, fried in a little oil until brown, then simmered or baked with tomato sauce for 35 to 40 minutes until cooked through.

Do you love chicken? Here are some tips for handling and cooking it.

How to Cook Chicken

Chicken is one of the most versatile meats on the planet. You can bake, boil, roast, grill, fry, sauté and use it about a hundred other ways.

Chicken is a cheap and nutritious meal. A chicken has eight main edible parts: two breasts, two thighs, two legs and two wings. The dark meat (leg and thigh) takes longer to cook. The white meat breast has fewer calories and fat.

Choosing Chicken
You can buy a whole chicken and roast it or buy chicken portions. Make sure that chicken skin is yellow or white and the package says Grade A poultry.
Check the package. Avoid leaky packages that are not well sealed. If you don't plan on cooking it right away, freeze it until later.

Handling Chicken
Raw chicken is a source of Salmonella. This type of bacteria can be deadly not destroyed through thorough cooking. So, how you handle raw poultry is very important.
Keep raw chicken isolated from other foods. Wherever you prepare it, wash up thoroughly with soap and hot water after the chicken is in the

oven. Wash your hands after the handling so you don't spread any bacteria. Avoid placing cooked chicken on the same chopping board as raw chicken.

Cooking Chicken

You can cook chicken in a variety of ways. Let's talk about roasting. Be sure to remove the bag of innards (heart, neck and gizzard) from the inside of the chicken before cooking. Season the inside and outside of the chicken for better flavour.
To hold in moisture, use a marinade or lightly cover the skin of the chicken with olive oil.
Cover with a tented piece of foil for most of the cooking. When there are about 15 or 20 minutes left, uncover so that the skin can brown.
Check the chicken is cooked through with no signs of blood before removing from the oven. Wait at least five minutes before cutting the chicken after it is done. This allows it to rest and the juices to permeate through the meat for even flavouring. Cutting too soon will spill all the juices and leave your meat dry.
No matter what the method of cooking, bone-in chicken will take longer to cook than boneless portions. Take this into account when gauging cooking times. To hold in moisture for boneless dishes, cover chicken during cooking. After cooking, refrigerate chicken no later than two hours afterwards.

Light Chicken Stew

2 tbsp sunflower oil
400g boneless, skinless chicken thighs, trimmed
and cut into chunks
1 onion, finely chopped
3 carrots, finely chopped
3 celery sticks, finely chopped
2 thyme sprigs or ½ tsp dried
1 bay leaf, fresh or dried
600ml vegetable or chicken stock

Heat the oil in a large pan, add the chicken, and
then fry until lightly browned. Add the
vegetables, and then fry for a few minutes more.
Stir in the herbs and stock. Bring to the boil. Stir
well, reduce the heat, then cover and cook for 40
minutes, until the chicken is tender.

Lemon Chicken

Ingredients:
For the chicken
150ml/5½fl oz chicken stock
2 lemons, zest and juice
1 garlic clove, left whole
4 x 150g/5½oz chicken breasts, skin removed

For the lemon sauce
250ml/9fl oz chicken stock
4 tbsp honey
4 lemons, zest and juice
Salt and freshly ground black pepper
75g/2¾oz butter

For the chicken, mix together the chicken stock, lemon zest and juice, and garlic clove in a large casserole. Bring to the boil, and then reduce the heat until the mixture is just simmering.

Add the chicken breasts and cover the casserole with a lid. Cook for 20-25 minutes, or until cooked through. Set aside to cool slightly.

For the lemon sauce, bring the chicken stock, honey and lemon zest and juice to the boil in a pan, and then continue to cook for 4-5 minutes to reduce a little.
Season, to taste, with salt and freshly ground black pepper.

Heat the butter in a frying pan over a medium heat. Add the cooled chicken breasts and fry for 2-3 minutes on each side, or until golden-brown on both sides.

To serve, place one chicken breast onto each of four serving plates. Pour over the lemon sauce.

Nice served with cauliflower rice.

Chicken, Watercress And Orange Salad

Ingredients:
1 chicken breast fillet
Salt and freshly ground black pepper
1 tbsp olive oil

For the salad:
1 small bunch of watercress, washed
1 orange, peeled, cut into segments
1 tbsp olive oil
1 tsp lemon juice

Preheat the oven to 220C/425F/Gas 7.
Heat the olive oil in a small ovenproof frying pan and season the chicken with salt and freshly ground black pepper.

Add the chicken and fry for two minutes, then turn over and transfer to the oven to roast for 10-12 minutes, or until completely cooked through. Remove and let cool.
When cool enough to handle shred the chicken into small pieces.

To serve, place the cooked chicken, watercress, orange, oil and lemon juice into a large bowl and mix well.

Chicken Tagine

This is one of my favourite dishes, and I make up and keep a spice pot using the dry spices in the paste recipe just for sprinkling onto any plain meat steaks I am frying up for a quick meal.

Ingredients:
For the paste:
2 Spanish onions
5 cloves garlic
1 lemon, juiced
1 bunch flat leaf parsley
1 bunch coriander
Sea salt, to season
Cumin powder, coriander powder, chilli powder and turmeric powder, to taste
½ cup extra virgin olive oil

For the chicken:
Olive oil, for cooking
1 chicken portion per person
1 Spanish onion, chopped into six
2 carrots, chopped into large pieces
2 tbsp honey
Small handful black olives
Water or stock
8 fresh dates, stones removed

To make the paste, place all the first list of ingredients in a food processor and blend.

Marinate the chicken well in the paste, leave overnight if possible.

Heat the olive oil in a heavy-based saucepan.
Add the chicken pieces and sauté for a couple of minutes, browning well on all sides.
Add the honey, vegetables, and olives and mix well.
Add enough stock or water to cover the chicken and vegetables, and braise until the chicken is cooked through and the vegetables are soft. Stir in the dates.

There should be enough here to feed 4 to 6 people, or you could freeze down the extra portions for use another time.

Rosemary Chicken With Tomato Sauce

1 tbsp olive oil
8 boneless, skinless chicken thighs
1 rosemary sprig, leaves finely chopped
1 red onion, finely sliced
3 garlic cloves, sliced
2 anchovy fillets, chopped
400g can chopped tomatoes
1 tbsp caper, drained

Heat half the oil in a non-stick pan, and then brown the chicken all over. Add half the chopped rosemary, stir to coat, and then set aside on a plate.
In the same pan, heat the rest of the oil, and then gently cook the onion for about 5 minutes until soft. Add the garlic, anchovies and remaining rosemary, and then fry for a few minutes more until fragrant. Pour in the tomatoes and capers with 75ml of water. Bring to the boil, and then return the chicken pieces to the pan. Cover, and then cook for 20 minutes until the chicken is cooked through. Season and serve with a crisp green salad.

Spicy Chicken with Vegetable Sauce

Ingredients:
For the spicy chicken
4 chicken breasts or thighs
2 cloves garlic, crushed
1 lemon, juice only
1 heaped tsp paprika
1 tsp ground cumin
Pinch cayenne pepper
1 tsp turmeric
Sea salt and freshly ground black pepper, to taste
1 tbsp olive oil, for griddling

For the vegetable sauce
2 tbsp olive oil
1 clove garlic, crushed
1 aubergine, chopped
1 red onion, chopped
2 courgettes, chopped
1 red pepper, seeds removed, flesh chopped
1 x 400g/14oz can chopped tomatoes
Sprig fresh oregano, finely chopped leaves only
Small handful flat leaf parsley, chopped
1 lemon, grated zest only

For the spicy chicken, mix all of the ingredients for the spicy chicken, apart from the olive oil, together in mixing bowl and mix to ensure the chicken is completely coated in the ingredients. Marinade for at least three hours or overnight.

To cook the chicken, heat a griddle pan until hot, then remove the chicken from the marinade and rub all over with the olive oil. Place on the griddle and cook for about 15 minutes for breast, 20 minutes for thighs, turning once or twice, or until cooked through (juices should run clear).

For the vegetable sauce, heat the olive oil in a wide pan over a medium heat and fry the garlic for one minute until soft. Add the aubergine, onion, courgettes and red pepper to the pan and fry for 20 minutes, stirring regularly until the vegetables are softened.

Stir in the tomatoes and oregano and cook for a further 20 minutes until reduced and thick.

In a small bowl mix together the parsley and lemon zest then stir this through the vegetables and serve with the griddled chicken.

Mushroom-Stuffed Chicken

25g dried porcini mushrooms, soaked in 250ml
water for 30 minutes, soaking liquid reserved
1 tbsp olive oil
1 onion, finely chopped
150g pack baby button mushrooms, finely
chopped
2 thyme sprigs, leaves removed and chopped
175ml water

Heat oven to 180C/fan 160C/gas 4. First, make
the stuffing. Finely chop the soaked porcini and
set aside. Heat the oil in a shallow pan, and then
gently cook the onion for 5 minutes, stirring
occasionally. Add the porcini, button mushrooms
and thyme leaves, season, turn the heat up, then
cook for another 5 minutes until the mushrooms
have softened.
Add the water to the pan, and then reduce fiercely
until nearly dry. Add 50ml of the porcini soaking
liquid, then continue to reduce for a couple of
minutes until you have a syrupy sauce. Allow to
cool for a couple of minutes, and then carefully
spoon between the skin and the flesh of the
chicken breasts.

Can be made a day ahead and chilled, or frozen
for 1 month. Defrost in fridge before cooking.
Season, place on a baking tray, skin-side up, then
cook in the oven for 20 minutes, until the chicken
is cooked through and golden.

Moroccan-Style Chicken With Carrot & Orange Salad

2 tsp ground cinnamon
1 tsp each cumin and coriander
1 tbsp olive oil
1 onion, thinly sliced
3 tbsp pine nuts
3 tbsp raisins
Juice 1 lemon
8 boneless, skinless chicken thighs

Salad:
400g carrots, coarsely grated
2 oranges
Mixed salad leaves
Handful chopped coriander

Heat oven to 190C/fan 170C/gas 5. Mix 1 tsp of the cinnamon with the cumin and coriander in a small bowl. Heat the oil in a frying pan, add the onion, and then quickly fry until lightly coloured. Add the pine nuts, and then fry until lightly toasted. Stir in ½ the spice mix, the raisins and the juice of ½ the lemon. Heat through, stirring, then remove from the heat.

Open out the chicken thighs and spoon a little stuffing onto each. Fold the chicken meat over to enclose the stuffing, then secure each thigh with a couple of cocktail sticks. Place in a non-stick roasting tin with the cocktail sticks underneath, then sprinkle with the remaining lemon juice and spice mix. Bake for 30-35 minutes until the chicken is tender and golden.

To make the salad, tip the carrot into a bowl. Using a sharp knife, remove the zest and pith from the oranges, and then cut into segments between membranes. Do this over the bowl to catch the juice, letting the segments drop in. Sprinkle with the reserved cinnamon and a little black pepper, and then mix well.

Divide the salad leaves between 4 plates, spoon over the salad, then sprinkle over the coriander leaves. Place the chicken alongside and serve.

Lamb Dishes

Lamb is another delicious meat that is popular amongst British people. Traditional Sunday roasts are often Roast Lamb with potatoes and vegetables and lashings of gravy made with the meat juices and scrapings from the roasting tin.

You can make it gluten free by not adding any bread based stuffing, or thickening the meat juices with wheat flour or corn flour, and not having Yorkshire puddings on the side.

Making the meal Paleo friendly would involve the above tips, plus eliminating the traditional roast potatoes or mash potatoes that often accompany the roast.

If you really cannot do without a good dollop of mash, why not substitute the mash for pureed swede or turnip. A good faux mash can be achieved by putting a fresh head of cauliflower through a food processor to 'rice' it, then gently steaming the riced cauliflower in the microwave with a little water until done.

Here follow a few tasty recipes using lamb.

Braised Lamb

Ingredients
½ leg of lamb
2 onions, sliced
3 cloves of garlic
24 cherry tomatoes
Small bunch of thyme
Olive oil
3 bay leaves
Black olives, stoned
½ bottle good red wine
150ml/5fl oz lamb stock

Sear the lamb in a casserole dish in the hot olive oil until well browned.
Remove and add the onion and garlic and tomatoes.
Cook for a minute or two and add the lamb.
Add the stock, red wine, bay leaves and olives and thyme.
Cover and cook in the oven at 180/350/Gas 4 for two hours. The lamb should be almost falling off the bone.

Serve with your choice of seasonal vegetables.

Warm Lamb Salad

Ingredients
250g/9oz lamb loin steak
Olive oil
Salt and black pepper
2 garlic cloves, crushed
2 sprigs rosemary
75g/3oz walnut halves
75g/3oz baby spinach, blanched
Handful flat leaf parsley, chopped
1 tbsp balsamic vinegar

Preheat the oven to 200C/400F/Gas 6.
Rub the lamb with the olive oil and season well
with salt and black pepper.
Heat a small ovenproof frying pan until hot, then
place the lamb, garlic and rosemary into the pan
and sear for 2-3 minutes on each side.
Transfer the pan to the oven and cook for ten
minutes or until cooked but slightly pink in the
middle.
Place the lamb onto a plate and cut into slices,
then add all of the remaining salad ingredients to
a bowl and mix well to combine.
To serve, place the mixed salad onto a serving
plate, then place the lamb on top of the salad.

Fruity Lamb Tagine

2 tbsp olive oil
500g lean diced lamb
1 large onion, roughly chopped
2 large carrots, quartered lengthways and cut into chunks
2 garlic cloves, finely chopped
2 tbsp spice mix:
(Mix a spoon of these together and keep in an empty spice pot: cardamom, cinnamon, clove, coriander, cumin, nutmeg, turmeric and black pepper)
400g can chopped tomatoes
200g dried apricots
600ml chicken stock

Heat oven to 180C/160C fan/gas 4. Heat the oil in a casserole and brown the lamb on all sides. Scoop the lamb out onto a plate, then add the onion and carrots and cook for 2-3 minutes until golden. Add the garlic and cook for 1 min more. Stir in the spices and tomatoes, and season. Tip the lamb back in with the apricots. Pour over the stock, stir and bring to a simmer. Cover the dish and place in the oven for 1 hr.
If the lamb is still a little tough, give it 20 minutes more until tender. When ready, leave it to rest so it's not piping hot, and then serve.

Roast Hogget

Hogget is meat from a sheep between one and two years old. It is absolutely delicious, and usually cheaper than spring lamb.

Part-boned and rolled leg or shoulder of hogget
1 tbsp olive oil
Small bunch of rosemary, broken into sprigs
3 garlic cloves, thinly sliced
4 anchovies, broken into small pieces (optional)

Heat oven 220C/200C fan/gas 7. Weigh the meat and calculate the cooking time: 15 minutes per 450g for rare, 20 minutes for medium and 25 minutes for well done.

Place the meat in a roasting tray, rub all over with the oil and season generously with salt and pepper. Use the tip of a sharp knife to make incisions all over the joint, and then in each one insert sprigs of rosemary with a sliver of garlic and piece of anchovy, if using. Put the meat in the oven for 10 minutes, and then turn down to 180C/160C fan/gas 4.

Now roast for your calculated time, basting the meat occasionally with any pan juices. Remove from the oven and rest the joint for at least 15 minutes before carving.

Greek Lamb Stew

This is enough for one person, so multiply the recipe to suit the number of people you are cooking for, or to make extra portions for freezing.

Ingredients
1 tbsp olive oil
100g/3½oz lamb, cubed
1 garlic clove, finely chopped
½ green pepper, chopped
1 tomato, chopped
8-10 black olives
2 tbsp red wine
200ml/7fl oz beef stock
1 sprig fresh rosemary

Heat the olive oil in a large saucepan. Add the lamb meat and fry for 3-4 minutes, stirring occasionally, until golden brown all over, then remove and set aside.
Add the garlic to the pan and cook for one minute in the lamb juices, then add the pepper, tomato, olives and red wine. Bring to the boil and cook for 1-2 minutes.
Add lamb pieces back to the pan along with the beef stock and rosemary, then reduce the heat and simmer for ten minutes, or until the lamb is cooked and tender.
Pour into a bowl and serve.

Spicy Lamb Curry

This does take a little bit more preparation, but the end results are well worth the extra time taken. This recipe will make about 5 to 6 portions.

Ingredients
For the curry paste
7.5cm/3in piece of fresh ginger, peeled and roughly chopped
7-8 garlic cloves, peeled and chopped
1 medium-sized onion, finely chopped

For the spice mix
1 tbsp ground coriander
1 tbsp cumin seeds
1 tbsp brown mustard seeds
½ tsp ground turmeric
1 tsp cayenne pepper

Extras:
3 tbsp vegetable oil
1kg/2¼lb boneless lamb cut into bite-size pieces
2 medium red onions, cut into thin rings
1¾-2 tsp salt

Put the ginger, garlic and onion for the curry paste in an electric blender along with 100ml/3½fl oz water. Blend to a fine paste.

Put the ingredients for the spice mix into a clean coffee grinder, or pestle and mortar. Grind to a fine powder.

Heat the oil in a large, wide, preferably non-stick, pan over a high heat. When hot, put in the lamb. Stir-fry for 10-15 minutes or until the lamb pieces brown. Reduce the heat to medium and add the curry paste and the spice mix. Stir once or twice to mix well. Add 500ml/17fl oz water and bring to the boil. Cover, turn the heat to low and cook for 45 minutes. Add the onion rings and salt to taste. Stir to mix. Cover and cook for a further 15-20 minutes, until the sauce is thick enough to coat the lamb.

Cooking Mackerel And Other Oily Fish.

We live on an island surrounded by the sea, so naturally we should make use of the abundant range of fish swimming around our coast. Ancient man ate fish and shellfish quite often, as can be seen in the prehistoric remains found in caves along our shores.

One of the most under used, and one of the tastiest fish in our seas is mackerel. Simple, quick methods of cooking are best for mackerel. Roasting, grilling or barbecuing all work well as the oils self-baste during cooking (pan-frying can cause the skin to stick to the pan).

Fruit works well with the oiliness of mackerel and it is traditionally served with a sharp sauce, such as gooseberry or rhubarb. It is also excellent cooked with oriental flavours, particularly ginger, lime, coriander and spices.

You don't want to end up with overcooked fish. Fish will go from translucent to opaque. You will see it turn white. This is another sign that you fish has reached doneness. At the first sign of opacity, remove the fish from the oven. It will continue to cook in the pan anyway and you don't want it to dry out and overcook.

Also note that some fish have pin bones. These are small bones left behind during filleting. The larger ones are removed but smaller ones can a nuisance for some. They can be removed with tweezers before cooking by pressing the meat with your fingers.

Cooking Fish

You can bake, roast, fry, microwave, steam or grill fish. Either way you choose, it will take careful attention to avoid overcooking.
Thin fillets will cook faster and may not need turning. Thicker ones can be turned halfway through the cooking process.
Roasting takes place at a slightly warmer temperature. Again watch the fish to be sure that it is cooking evenly.
If you grill a fish steak, use a sheet of tin foil to cover the grill. This helps prevent it from falling apart between the grate and ruining your meal.

Salmon Burgers

4 boneless, skinless salmon fillets, about
550g/1lb 4oz in total, cut into chunks
2 tbsp Thai red curry paste
Thumb-size piece fresh root ginger, grated
1 bunch coriander, half chopped, half leaves
picked
1 tsp olive oil
Lemon wedges, to serve

Tip the salmon into a food processor with the
paste, ginger and chopped coriander. Pulse until
roughly minced. Tip out the mix and shape into 4
burgers. Heat the oil in a non-stick frying pan,
then fry the burgers for 4-5 minutes on each side,
turning until crisp and cooked through.

Smoked Salmon With Prawns, Horseradish & Lime Vinaigrette

1 tsp horseradish sauce
4 slices smoked salmon
10 large cooked prawns, peeled but tails left on

Vinaigrette:
Juice 1 lime, finely grated zest of ½
1 tsp clear honey
½ tsp finely grated fresh root ginger
2 tbsp light olive oil
2 handfuls small leaf salad

For the dressing, whisk the limejuice and zest with the honey, ginger and seasoning, then whisk in the oil. Lay the smoked salmon and prawns on 2 plates.

Toss the salad in most of the dressing and pile on top. Drizzle the remaining dressing around the plate and serve with a little horseradish sauce on the side.

Baked Salmon With Fennel & Tomatoes

2 medium fennel bulbs
2 tbsp chopped flat-leaf parsley
Zest and juice 1 lemon
175g cherry tomatoes
1 tbsp olive oil
2 salmon fillets, about 175g each
Few black olives (optional)

Heat oven to 180C/fan 160C/gas 4.
Trim the fronds from the fennel and set aside.
Cut the fennel bulbs in half, and then cut each
half into 3 wedges. Cook in boiling salted water
for 10 minutes, and then drain well.
Chop the fennel fronds roughly, and then mix
with the parsley and lemon zest.
Spread the drained fennel over a shallow
ovenproof dish, and then add the tomatoes.
Drizzle with olive oil, and then bake for 10
minutes. Nestle the salmon among the
vegetables, sprinkle with lemon juice, then bake
15 minutes more until the fish is just cooked.
Scatter over the parsley and serve.

Charred Salmon With Fennel & Olive Salad

2 large fennel bulbs
6 ripe tomatoes
Zest and juice 1 lemon
3 tbsp extra-virgin olive oil, plus extra to serve
100g black olives, pitted
1 tbsp capers, drained
600g piece salmon fillet, skin on and scaled
1 tbsp vegetable oil
2 x 20g packs flat-leaf parsley, leaves roughly chopped

If you are lucky enough to get a fennel bulb with fronds, pick them off and keep them. Trim the fennel and slice it as thinly as possible. Bring a large pan of salted water to the boil, and have a bowl of iced water ready. Tip the fennel into the pan, leave for 30 seconds, then lift into the iced water with a slotted spoon.

Roughly chop the tomatoes. Put a sieve over a large bowl and squeeze the seeds and juice from the tomatoes with your hands. Get rid of the seeds but keep the juices ready to make the dressing. Add the lemon zest and juice, olive oil and a good pinch of salt to the tomato juices and stir well. Drain the fennel well and add to the bowl along with the olives, capers and the tomato flesh. Mix well, and then set aside.

Heat oven to 180C/160C fan/gas 4. Cut the salmon into 4 fillets, rub well with the vegetable oil and season with salt and pepper. Heat a griddle or frying pan with an ovenproof handle, then cook the salmon, skin-side down, over a medium heat for 7 minutes. There may be some smoke, but what is important is that the salmon is well charred so it has a bitter, crisp bottom and the flesh is sweet, soft and almost translucent inside. Now pop the salmon into the oven, still skin-side down in the pan, and then roast for 3 minutes until just cooked through.

Roughly chop the parsley and mix through the salad. Serve the salad on plates, then carefully lift the salmon from the pan and sit it on top, skin-side up. Drizzle with a little more extra virgin olive oil and serve.

Mackerel & Beetroot Salad

3 smoked mackerel fillets, skinned
250g pack cooked beetroot
100g bag mixed salad leaves
2 celery sticks, finely sliced
50g walnut pieces

For the dressing:
Whisk together 3 tbsp olive oil, 1 tbsp lemon
juice and 1 tsp Dijon mustard
2 tsp creamed horseradish sauce

Flake the mackerel fillets into large pieces and
cut the beetroot into bite-size chunks.

Mix the salad dressing and horseradish sauce
together in a salad bowl and season.

Add the salad leaves, mackerel, beetroot, celery
and walnuts, and toss gently.

Barbecued Mackerel With Ginger, Chilli & Lime Drizzle

3 tbsp extra-virgin olive oil
4 small whole mackerel, gutted and cleaned

1 large red chilli, deseeded and finely chopped
1 small garlic clove, finely chopped
Small knob fresh root ginger, finely chopped
2 tsp honey
Finely grated zest and juice of 2 limes
1 tsp olive
1 tsp Thai fish sauce

Light the barbecue and allow the flames to die
down until the ashes have gone white with heat.
Make the drizzle by whisking 2 tbsp olive oil and
all the other ingredients together in a small bowl,
adjusting the ratio of honey and lime to make a
sharp sweetness. Season to taste.
Score each side of the mackerel about 6 times,
not quite through to the bone. Brush the fish with
the remaining oil and season lightly. Barbecue
the mackerel for 5-6 minutes on each side until
the fish is charred and the eyes have turned
white. Spoon the drizzle over the fish and allow
to stand for 2-3 minutes before serving.

Smoked Mackerel With Quick Grilled Ratatouille

Aubergine, halved lengthways and cut into strips
Courgette, cut into strips lengthways
2 red peppers, cut into strips lengthways
2 large tomatoes, cut into quarters
Extra-virgin olive oil
½ lime, juiced
50g rocket
4 smoked mackerel fillets, broken into large
pieces

Heat a griddle (char grill). Brush the vegetables
lightly with oil and grill for 2 minutes each side
until tender (do the tomatoes last as they will
stick a little).

Put the vegetables into a large bowl, season and
toss with the lime juice, a little more olive oil and
the rocket. Divide between four plates and serve
with the smoked mackerel.

Mackerel With Warm Cauliflower & Caper Salad

300g cauliflower, cut into florets
1 lemon
4 tsp capers, rinsed
½ small bunch flat-leaf parsley, chopped
½ small bunch mint, chopped
2 tsp olive oil
1 small garlic clove, crushed
2 large or 4 small mackerel fillets

Heat the grill and bring a pan of water to the boil.
Drop the cauliflower into the water, and then
cook for 4-5 minutes until just tender. Zest and
juice half the lemon, then mix with the capers,
parsley, mint, olive oil and garlic in a salad bowl.
When the cauliflower is cooked, drain, and then
stir into the herby dressing with some seasoning
while still hot.
Put the mackerel on a baking tray, zest the
remaining lemon half over it, season, then grill
for a couple of minutes on each side. Cut the
lemon into wedges. Serve alongside the mackerel
and cauliflower salad.

Grilled Mackerel With Orange, Chilli & Watercress Salad

1 tsp black peppercorns
1 tsp coriander seeds
4 oranges
1 red chilli, deseeded, finely chopped
8 fresh mackerel fillets
1 tsp wholegrain mustard
1 tbsp clear honey
120g bag watercress, spinach and rocket salad
mix
1 shallot , thinly sliced

Finely crush the peppercorns and coriander seeds
together using a pestle and mortar. Grate the zest
from half an orange and mix into the pepper
mixture with half the chopped chilli. Lightly
slash the skin of the mackerel and press the zesty,
peppery mixture onto the fish. Heat the grill.

For the salad, segment the oranges. First slice the
top and bottom off each orange, then cut away
the peel and any white pith using a small, sharp
knife. Holding each orange over a bowl to catch
all the juice, cut down either side of each
segment to release it, then squeeze the shells to
release any extra juice. Measure 4 tbsp of this
juice into a small bowl and mix with the mustard,
honey and remaining chilli.
Grill the mackerel, skin-side up, for 4 minutes or
until crisp and cooked through. Meanwhile,

divide the salad leaves between 4 plates and scatter with the orange segments and sliced shallot. Drizzle with the chilli orange dressing and top with the grilled mackerel.

Sardines Stuffed With Orange Slices & Bay Leaves

4 large sardines or 8 small, scaled and gutted
2 oranges, 1 thinly sliced and slices halved, and 1 juiced
4 bay leaves or 8, depending on the number of fish
Olive oil
Paprika, hot or sweet, to dust
½ cucumber, peeled and cut into chunks

Stuff the sardines with 2 or 3 slices of orange, a bay leaf and season well. Rub with a little oil and dust with paprika.

Heat the barbecue. Cook the sardines for a few minutes on each side (about 2 minutes for small ones and 4 for large ones). Check they are cooked by pulling the back fin - when they are ready it will come out easily. Squeeze over some orange juice. Dress the cucumber with the remaining orange juice, some sea salt and black pepper, and serve with the sardines.

Grilled Sardines With Cherry Tomatoes, Rocket & Fennel

1 bulb fennel, trimmed
8 small or 4 large sardines, gutted, cleaned and heads removed
A few sprigs thyme, leaves stripped
2 garlic cloves, peeled and thinly sliced
4 small bunches cherry tomatoes on the vine
Olive oil
100g wild rocket
A squeeze lemon juice

Slice the fennel as thinly as possible, preferably using a mandolin, then drop into a bowl of iced water. Leave to soak for about 20 minutes to allow the fennel to crisp up.
To flatten the sardines and remove the backbone, open out the gut cavity and lay the fish on the chopping board skin side up. Press down on the backbone with the palm of your hand from the head to the tail. Turn the fish over and peel off the backbone. If you need to, use a pair of scissors to cut it out. Don't worry if you have a few small bones remaining.

Heat the grill to the highest setting. Lay the sardines, skin side up, on an oiled baking tray. Season and scatter the thyme and garlic over. Lay the tomatoes on top. Drizzle with a little more oil and grill for 4-6 minutes, until cooked through.

Drain the fennel well and toss in a bowl with the rocket, lemon juice, 4 tbsp olive oil and some seasoning. Serve with the sardines.

Winter tuna Niçoise

2 tbsp olive oil
4 eggs
1 tbsp lemon juice
2 tbsp caper, rinsed
50g Sun Blush or sundried tomatoes in oil, finely
chopped
½ red onion, thinly sliced
100g baby spinach
2 x 160g or 200g tins yellow fin tuna steak,
drained

Put eggs in a small pan of water, bring to the boil,
and then simmer for 8-10 minutes, depending on
how you like them cooked. Plunge into a bowl of
cold water to cool for a few minutes. Peel away
the shells, then cut into halves.
In a large salad bowl, whisk together the oil,
lemon juice, capers and chopped tomatoes.
Season, tip in the onion, spinach, and tuna, and
then gently toss together. Top with the eggs, then
serve straight away.

Sauces Condiments and Crudités

Needless to say we all like a little bit of sauce to liven up some meals, especially those that are not cooked in sauces or gravy that are part of the meal like curry or stew.

Sometimes we would just like a simple snack of vegetable crudités with a dip when we are peckish, and a full cooked meal is not called for.

So here are a few gluten-free, Paleo friendly ideas for you

For crudités try these ideas:
Lightly cooked asparagus tips
Flat or runner beans, topped, tailed and cut diagonally
Individual leaves of red or white endive/chicory
Individual leaves of little gem lettuce
Whole radishes, with the stalk attached
Baby turnips, raw or lightly cooked
Scrubbed baby carrots
Thickly sliced fennel

Anchovy Dip

Ingredients
60g/2½oz anchovy fillets, roughly chopped
4 cloves garlic, roughly chopped
2 shallots, roughly chopped
1 tbsp red wine vinegar
Handful parsley, finely chopped
150ml/5fl oz extra virgin olive oil
Freshly ground black pepper

To make the dip, put all the ingredients except
the olive oil and black pepper in a processor, and
switch on. Pour the oil into the blender in a
steady stream, until it forms a thick sauce.
Pour into a pan and heat through. Season with
freshly ground black pepper and serve
immediately.

Guacamole

1 red onion, finely chopped
1 tbsp of ground coriander
1 tbsp of ground cumin
8 ripe Hass avocados
3 red chilli, seeded and finely chopped
Juice of 3 lemons
2 tbsp freshly chopped chives
Salt and pepper to taste

In a large bowl combine the red onion, coriander
and cumin.
Add the avocados to the bowl and mash well with
a fork until smooth.
Add the chillies, lemon and season generously
with salt and pepper, and mix well. Sprinkle with
the chopped chives and serve.

Basil And Spinach Pesto

Ingredients
2 handfuls spinach leaves
55g/2oz pine nuts, toasted
Small bunch fresh basil leaves
5 tbsp olive oil
Salt and freshly ground black pepper

Blend all of the pesto ingredients in a food processor to a paste. Add more olive oil as necessary to loosen the mixture.

To serve, place in a bowl with a plate of crudités on the side.

Parsley Pesto

2 tbsp olive oil
A handful of fresh parsley
1 tbsp whole almonds
Salt and black pepper
Squeeze of lemon juice

Place all the parsley pesto ingredients into a small food processor and blend until smooth.

This is nice spread over a plain roast chicken breast.

Coriander Pesto

3 tbsp olive oil
Salt and black pepper
1 garlic clove, chopped
2 handfuls fresh coriander leaves

Place all of the ingredients into a food processor
and pulse until smooth.

This comes in handy to flavour a quick carrot
soup, or mix through plain boiled vegetables to
liven up any meal.

Gluten-Free Desserts That Are Paleo Friendly And Not Too Expensive!

The whole emphasis behind the Paleo diet is to break away from manufactured and heavily processed foods that often contain a lot of sugar.

Sugar comes in many forms so you have to read packet ingredients carefully. The usual rule of thumb is to look for any ingredients that end in 'ose' such as sucrose, lactose, fructose etc. These are all sugar under a different name.

Pretty much the only sugar a hunter-gatherer would come across would be want was naturally contained in fruit and berries, as well as the occasional honeycomb he would gather. These sources of sugar would have come with the perfect balance of vitamins and fibre you find in the whole product, and our bodies are able to cope well with consuming sugar in its natural form.

Your average cave man didn't wander the plains or scale hills while sucking his way through a packet of sugar free mints either, so anything that contains artificial sweeteners would also be a no-no on the Paleo diet.

Anyone following a gluten-free diet that is not quite so bothered by the ethical side of things may be happy to use a sweetener in their tea in place of sugar, but if you must have your tea sweetened, then a little natural honey will be a lot more gentle on your system that the chemical makeup of these artificial sweeteners.

Personally, I like nothing more than a cup of Earl Grey with a slice of lemon and a small dash of honey. I really don't miss the milk at all!

So, onto dessert and if you really must round off your meal with something sweet, then why not try a fresh orange, or crisp apple sliced up and served with a few raisins. But if you want something a little more elegant or decadent, then try the following ideas.

Sweet Grilled Oranges

Grilled oranges are simple and inexpensive to make, yet the flavour is rich and delicious.

They can be eaten as a light dessert. I prefer them cooked on a freshly cleaned grill as to keep the distinct contrast of the citrus and sweet. If you prefer though, you can cook them after you've grilled some flavourful meat and they will take on a light smoky flavour.

Ingredients:
2 – 4 large oranges
Honey
Cinnamon, ground

Amounts will vary depending on how many oranges you use and how sweet you want the end results to be.

Preparation:
Cut the oranges into approximately ¼ inch thick slices. You can do this with the rind on or if you prefer, you can first peel the oranges. I tend to cook two oranges at a time and to leave the rind on as they tend to be easier to flip.
Preheat the grill to a low temperature. Brush the grate with a little olive oil to keep the fruit from sticking.

Place the orange slices on the warm grill and allow them to cook about 5 minutes. Flip them over and continue cooking another 3 minutes.

Once they begin to soften, drizzle with honey and sprinkle over a little cinnamon to taste, and allow to cook for another minute or two.

Remove from grill. Best served warm.

Baked Apple

Ingredients
1 apple, cored
Sprinkle of ground cinnamon
A drizzle of honey
4 damsons

Pre-heat the oven to 220C/425F/Gas 7.
Place the apple onto a non-stick baking tray.
Sprinkle with cinnamon and then drizzle the
honey over.
Scatter with damsons and bake in the oven for
10-15 minutes.
Serve warm.

Baked Apple With Butter

Ingredients
For the baked apple
55g/2oz raisins
30g/1oz butter
1 tbsp clear honey
1 orange, zest only
1 apple, cored

For the baked apple, place the raisins, butter, honey and orange zest into a small bowl and mix well.

Place the apple onto a microwave-proof plate and stuff the raisin mixture into the hole left by removing the core.
Cook in the microwave on high for 3½ minutes, or until softened.

Spiced Peaches

Ingredients
2 tins of peach halves in juice
1 tbsp white wine vinegar
3 tbsp runny honey
2 short sticks cinnamon
4cm/1½in piece fresh ginger, peeled and sliced
thinly into rounds
½ tsp dried chilli flakes
¼ tsp salt
¼ tsp whole black peppercorns
3 cloves

Empty the cans of peaches with their juice into a
saucepan.
Add the vinegar, honey, cinnamon, sliced ginger,
chilli flakes, salt, peppercorns and cloves.
Bring to the boil and let it bubble for a minute or
so, then turn off the heat and leave in the pan to
keep warm.
Serve warm.

Warm Fruit Compote

4 tablespoons runny honey
3 wide strips of orange zest
1 vanilla pod, split lengthways
140g cooked chestnuts
100g dried cherries
100g dried apricots

Put the honey, orange zest and vanilla in a pan
with 200ml water. Bring to the boil, stirring to
dissolve the honey, then add the chestnuts and
dried fruits. Simmer, uncovered, for 10 minutes
until the sauce is slightly thickened. Leave to
cool a little, remove the vanilla pod, then serve
warm.

Thank you for buying our book – we hope you enjoy the recipes within, and can find some favourite ones that you will use often in your cooking.

Suggested further reading:

Enjoy Your Holiday Feast On A Low Carb Diet: Special Report - How To Do Low Carb Holidays by Budding Books - Kindle eBook available via Amazon

Enjoy Your Holiday Feast On A Low Carb Diet: Don't Sacrifice A Thing With These Delicious Dishes by Budding Books - Kindle eBook available via Amazon

Delicious Gourmet Garden Salad Recipes: Creative Ways With Your Home Grown Produce by Budding Books - Kindle eBook available via Amazon

Gourmet Garden Salads Harvest Goodness From Plant To Plate by Budding Books - Kindle eBook available via Amazon

Eating To Lose Weight: Adding The Right Foods To Promote Weight Loss by Budding Books - Kindle eBook available via Amazon

Eating To Lose Weight: Adding The Right Foods To Promote Weight Loss 30 Delicious and

Healthy Recipes by Budding Books - Kindle eBook available via Amazon

Frugal Family Chicken Recipes: Cheap Recipes To Stretch The Family Food Budget by Budding Books - Kindle eBook available via Amazon

11 Of The Most Popular Diets Demystified by Budding Books - Kindle eBook available via Amazon

Printed in Great Britain
by Amazon.co.uk, Ltd.,
Marston Gate.